YELLOW PAPER DAISY

QWA-SA SPELT WRONG

COMMANDER RO

Made with ♥ on the Notion Press Platform
www.notionpress.com

To all great lovers, lost in love and lost love.

This ode to the rhythms of the heart shall never stop,

So shall we.

Go on loving, for there is no greater purpose.

Contents

Preface *xi*

Acknowledgements *xiii*

Prologue *xv*

To Be

1. Angels' Cries 3
2. Glance 4
3. Wants And Needs 5
4. Control 6
5. Conversation 7
6. One Last Time 8
7. Desperation 9
8. Crave 10
9. Assure 11
10. Certify 12
11. Her And Her Beauty 13
12. Deep In My Head 14
13. Singular Thought 15
14. Sleep Over 16
15. Holler 17
16. Ease 18
17. Silly 19
18. Cessation 20
19. Availability 21
20. Care Less? 22

Contents

21. Over Again 23
22. Heart's Fire 24
23. Hurt 25
24. Why Not Turn Around? 26
25. At Your Disposal 27
26. You And Always You 28
27. An Undying Wish 29
28. Mountain Through Time 30
29. Stability 31
30. Assertion 32
31. The Realest Sun 33
32. Tear Down 34
33. Yearn 35
34. Never A Lost Memory 36
35. You & I 37
36. Termination 38
37. Indemnify 39
38. Censure 40
39. Delusion 41
40. Lost In The Head 42
41. Substantial Exchange 43
42. Precedence 44
43. Dependence 45
44. Competence 46

Contents

45. Supposition 47

46. The Only Dream 48

47. Desire 49

48. Wings 50

49. You In My Head 51

50. Either You Or Nothing 52

51. Commiserate 53

52. A Losing Battle 54

53. Part Ways 55

54. Avarice 56

55. Lost Love 57

56. Jones 58

57. Benevolence 59

58. Loss 60

59. Cringey? 61

60. Me And My Thoughts 62

Not To Be

61. Hope 65

62. Now That It's No More 66

63. Restate 67

64. Confusion 68

65. A Pessimistic Heart 69

66. Awareness 70

67. Look Back 71

Contents

68. Grief 72

69. Progress 73

70. Ingredient Of Chaos 74

71. Madman 75

72. Expectation 76

73. Evocation 77

74. Giggle 78

75. Vanquish 79

76. A Fool's Thought 80

77. Longing 81

78. Restless 82

79. Proxy 83

80. Caution 84

81. Chimera 85

82. Recalcitrant 86

83. Anticipation 87

84. A Promise Of Euphoria 88

85. Closer But Never Closer 89

86. Eyes To See 90

87. Merit 91

88. Notability, Lack Of It 92

89. Prediction 93

90. Fantasy 94

91. Decent Down 95

Contents

92. Falsely Accused 96

93. A Greater Plan 97

94. Reckoning 98

95. Boundless, Barrierless 99

96. Notion 100

97. Unease 101

98. Me And My Sleep 102

99. Vexation 103

100. Worry 104

101. Thought Fit 105

102. Unsettled 106

103. Necessitate 107

104. Always You 108

105. Solitude 109

106. All Over Again 110

107. It's Me 111

108. Timeless 112

109. Lighthouse 113

110. Distraction 114

111. De Novo 115

112. Cupio 116

113. Prowess 117

114. It's Never Right 118

115. Xx(x)-wn 119

Contents

116. Stance	120
117. An Assignment Left Behind	121
118. Juger	122
119. Intact	123
120. Her And I	124

Preface

I had to pen down this book of poems, solely with one audience in mind.

The entire collection being more of a conversation with her at most than a publications at least, At the lack of the attention from this beautiful human being, I choose to let my thoughts out onto the pen and here is a product of such thoughts. Many men tried and failed and I shall be one more of them, But I am not a friend of fear to embrace this failure.

I cannot offer a greater number of words, but emotions.

This is mere art made to enjoy while your heart aches beyond bounds. I offer this to thee reader's eyes, for I hope a little joy is brought into the light within your heart.

"Blessed are the forgetful, for they get the better even of their blunders."

- Friedrich Nietzsche

Acknowledgements

My heartful thanks go to my dear sisters Janu and Ria for being the hardest critics through the history.

While you had your own battles to fight, no moment's hesitation was noticed when I needed a fresh set of eyes at my poems.

For more to come and mere happiness to be felt, An eternity of grace and remembrance.

Prologue

"'I wish to hold you close,

While you flap your wings,

For us to take a beautiful flight,

To reach the end of the world"

"Burn me at the heart of the infernal flames of hell,

Push me off the tallest mountain that stands high prideful,

Rest me in the silence of the cosmos to glide around,

I shall show no hesitation, if you promise to hold my hand in this life or the next."

"I wish to stand as the colossal of hope,

While a long wait for you to change your mind is set in place.

I wish to find peace with you,

Become a piece within you.""

To Be

1. Angels' Cries

Angels weep at the resonance of your beauty.
For all they can fathom,
Is the depth of your benevolence.
Radiating bright blues from the heart of the universe.

2. Glance

I feel as if my heart has a veil on it.
It seems to shrink at an uncontrollable rate,
When I lay my eyes on you.

3. Wants and Needs

The uncertainability of never being able,
To glare at your presence,
Makes me crave twice as much for you.
Makes me fumble twice as much than ever.

4. Control

I have words as my power.
I control, command, and confiscate the room,
With so much ease.
But with you around, I can only try.

5. Conversation

Either boredom,
Or over-flowing interest,
I miss your unforgiving rage,
To exchange words.

6. One last time

I have told myself, this would be the last time,
I would fall.
Out of them all, I want this to be the last,
The most.

7. Desperation

Nowhere throughout history,
I wanted the aspect of certainty, so desperately,
The aspect of your presence around me,
So desperately.

8. Crave

I would lay waste to such deepest desires in my heart,
Such desires that would bring down monarchies,
Or burn down kingdoms,
For your presence as an exchange.

9. Assure

I shall eternally be grateful,
Grateful at every chance I had,
To hold your hand and ensure you heard,
"I feel good."

10. Certify

Only if time was a friend,
Memory my acquaintance,
I would travel back and tell myself,
She is the one.

11. Her and Her beauty

A thousand suns etch my pupils,
When I glare into them eyes.
Yet not a moment's hesitation, I'd own,
To be blind.

12. Deep in my head

Pen block,
A poet's worst nightmare.
With you wandering my head,
Has no command over me.

13. Singular thought

I wonder,
Weather to blame you or myself.
For nothing but you walk the meadows of my imagination,
Throughout my day.

14. Sleep over

If a dream existed,
To defy the bounds of time,
To spend every waking moment with you,
I would never wake up.

15. Holler

I wish to stand at the top of the world,
To shout my lungs out,
"I miss you."
Where even the gods shall shiver to defy the worth of my compassion.

16. Ease

It can only get so easy with the burden of bearing love,
Easy at dealing ache,
Easy at being breathless,
Easy at being relentless,
Ease towards desperation.

17. Silly

If the sciences between the atoms' existence tell me,
I have never touched anything, Let alone you.
I would be adventurous enough,
To push those electrons closer.

18. Cessation

Patience, My arch nemesis,
I shall outlive you,
For her to change her mind.
I shall bear the singularity of conscience above you.

19. Availability

You alone have the power,
Over my downfall or a superior legacy.
And for all I see,
The only factor that determines either is your presence.

20. Care less?

I can only fight so many things.
As I ponder on the hope,
Of the liberation,
Of the constraints of the general eye lays on how I should love.

21. Over again

If only I can do all of this again,
I would change nothing but only do more of it.
Look at you more,
Listen to you more,
Hold your hands more,
Hold you closer more.

22. Heart's Fire

You enrage such deep emotions in my heart,
Those of which,
Consume my conscience,
Cripple my perspectives,
Command my attention,
Commend my motives.

23. Hurt

For the sake of love, I shall suffer.
Such excruciating pain, any man would wither down,
All at the hopes of walking this bed of thorns,
I shall gladly commute, the destination being your arms.

24. Why not turn around?

As the calm before the storm exists,
I own zen at its purity, before a hurricane of your thoughts hit,
The frequency going low by the day,
Only makes me want to get you back sooner.

25. At your disposal

If I die tomorrow,
Use my body as firewood to keep you warm.
If I forget you tomorrow,
Use my memories to know you have known love.
If you move on tomorrow,
I will ensure to use yours an outlet for my rage.

26. You and always You

Every day I wake,
Since your closest acquaintance,
I think of you,
And the same before my eyes lay to waste,
Where I spend endless euphoria for a dream,
With you in it.

27. An undying wish

I hope one day,
My cherry blossom,
You shall root down into my heart as I wish and breathe,
To blossom such beautiful flowers of passion,
For no man can defy our compassion.

28. Mountain through time

I wish to stand as the colossal of hope,
While a long wait for you to change your mind is set in place.
I wish to find peace with you,
Become a piece within you.

29. Stability

The only resort to my thoughts,
At the absence of anything not worthy of you, Is you.
Nothing comes to my mind but you,
When I am at my utmost peace,
And I wish the same lasts long.

30. Assertion

I stand prideful, with utmost confidence,
That you are the one.
For my other half of Androgynous,
Has been finally found,
We stand with victory over gods,
As such pride bestrides my heart when you rest in it.

31. The Realest Sun

A thousand suns,
Shall not even come close to the fire I own in my heart.
The fire's sole fuel being you,
The death of it, your disapproval.

32. Tear Down

Day by day, without you around,
My heart seems to gain more weight.
More as now to crush a mammoth,
More to come to crush the worlds.

33. Yearn

Such great pain is what I feel,
Lacking the greatest pleasure, I have known,
Rooting from your acquaintance,
I can only try and numb it, But the next day holds twice fold.

34. Never a lost memory

My deepest fear rooted in the darkest corners of my heart,
Stands forgetfulness.
Forgetfulness at the cost of pain, I implicate on myself of you,
So deep is the fear that I shall make up my mind to forget you.

35. You & I

I wish to exist above time and space with you.
Where puny world pleasures would hold no merit,
Where no other soul has a mouth to speak but us,
For all to hold dear is each other.

36. Termination

I hope this ends soon,
The distance,
The silence,
The search,
The pain,
The anticipation,
The hopelessness,
The tire,
The distance.

37. Indemnify

Burn me at the heart of the infernal flames of hell,
Push me off the tallest mountain that stands high prideful,
Rest me in the silence of the cosmos to glide around,
I shall show no hesitation, if you promise to hold my hand in
this life or the next.

38. Censure

Long and lonely evenings, I spend.
Wondering should I reach you.
Better would it have been an era of letters,
I would have blamed the postman for not delivering the mail.

39. Delusion

My tattoo's healed,
But my heart bleeds.
Come back, O'Dear.
My medicine, let us glue this heart back,
As though nothing happened to it.

40. Lost in the head

Staring at the walls has never been so not boring,
Interesting myself in my interests do not seem much interesting anymore.
You devil! How dare you deplete me of my guilty pleasures,
To replace them all with yourself.

41. Substantial Exchange

Your eyes, Over a million meteor showers,
Your hands, Over a campfire on a freezing night,
Your nagging, Over a Beethoven's symphony,
Your smile, Over the full bright moon,
You, over a million souls around the world.

42. Precedence

Can I tell the birds that fly your way,
A piece of my mind.
Can I feel your odour from the wind,
That flew my way through you.
Can I rewrite your priorities,
Make it Me, Myself & I.

43. Dependence

The thought that once we spent an entire evening,
Holding each other, Make me feel the warmth of home.
And I worry each passing day,
Would this addict rehabilitate from such a thing.

44. Competence

Every waking moment, I worry on the strength I own,
To again glue my heart back, after breaking it to a million pieces.
Such fear I own for the recurring process,
That can deplete me of all my energy to do it again.

45. Supposition

Death of my dream,
For you are a mere human, yet a deity to me.
Awareness I own of you prone to destruction,
Yet I ask the ideal outcome of you.
Such is the burden of responsibility I lay on you,
To do right by me.

46. The only dream

The reality does not seem so great about us,
Let me slide into that beautiful dream,
To walk the gardens of euphoria with you.
No bounds human made shall obstruct us.

47. Desire

I lay me heart at your feet, you ask the reason why!
I lay my pride aside, you ask why!
I hope not to tell my mind to lay my attention aside,
I hope to lay the burden of distance from thee, into nothingness.

48. Wings

I wish to hold you close,
While you flap your wings,
For us to take a beautiful flight,
To reach the end of the world.

49. You in my head

Hunger eludes me,
Sleep eludes me,
Sense eludes me,
Logic eludes me,
Time eludes me,
Pride eludes me,
Priorities elude me,
But not your thoughts.

50. Either you or Nothing

Guilt almost consumes me into nothingness,
At the smallest thought,
of opening my heart to another woman,
My heart seems to resist any worldly pleasure,
Which does not involve you.

51. Commiserate

My Yellow Paper daisy,
Do you have no mercy on this feeble heart,
If crushing it is what gives you happiness,
I would gladly live with half an organ.

52. A losing Battle

As much as I can fight,
My capability to resist the numbing of my emotions,
Seem to have set in place,
The longer you are away from me.

53. Part Ways

Every attempt at the wake of reaching you,
Every failed attempt,
Seems to consume a piece of my soul,
A piece forever lost,
To never feel a deeper emotion ever.

54. Avarice

Greed commands over my conscience,
For I no longer care, Yet still care of your priorities.
Whence my greed seeks nothing from you,
But you.

55. Lost love

Love lost heart seeks love found,
Once found, only to get back on the search.
Madman's tales to project sanity,
Innocent emotion to be sentenced to guilt,
Love lost shall be found.

56. Jones

The first step to tackle an addiction,
Is to completely accept helplessness.
And day after day,
I feel such helplessness in your absence,
Yet happy addicted to you.

57. Benevolence

How dare you fiddle with a heart as if it were your own,
How dare you blind me with your radiance,
How dare you silence me with your presence,
How dare your become prominent at my heart.

58. Loss

You beautiful vicious creature,
I miss the days we spent,
Where our only third wheel being joy,
I miss those days where your only resort to communicate,
Was me.

59. Cringey?

Surreal thoughts cloud my judgement,
Thoughts blazing enough to burn this world,
Such is the sacrifice, I would lay at your feet,
Before I lay on my back peaceful and cold.

60. Me and My thoughts

More the time flies away,
I stand to condescend my affection,
I stand to doubt your ever originated affection,
May I have turned a blind eye for what you are,
Rest assured, not a strand of compassion reduced,
And this thinker thinks.

Not To Be

61. Hope

Even at the verge of losing it all,
I still stand hopeful,
Love has blinded me beyond comprehension,
Or to simply look beyond logic.

62. Now that it's no more

I feel more ease now,
Despite the door forever shut,
Yet I still choose not to accept defeat.
For I want to go on to shut my heart towards any other worldly pleasure.

63. Restate

Thinking of you before shutting my eye,
To thinking of you to lose my sleep,
If I am asked to do it all again,
I shall gladly do so.

64. Confusion

Even at the break you give me,
I choose to read between the lines,
To get back along and never alone someday,
Either I am love sick or you stupid to make me understand.

65. A Pessimistic Heart

I go concocting more plans,
Which lack sanity,
Yet partially wonder,
Would the achievement be as thrilling as the pursuit.

66. Awareness

You choose to bear the audacity,
To tell me that I do not know you,
I might not be so educated,
on the events that moulded you,
Yet, I see you clear.

67. Look back

Curiosity clouds my sadness,
But one happy ride, It was.
For I am glad we denied to turn rivals,
Rather strangers.

68. Grief

I wondered it was close to impossible,
To pass my day,
if your presence was no longer accessible.
I stand surprised beyond comprehension,
To be wrong.
Yet a feeling of having to lost,
Something prominent runs my mind.

69. Progress

I wondered the boulder would roll off my heart,
Once you paid more attention.
It rather is being sculpt to nothingness,
Now that you are lost at all cost.

70. Ingredient of Chaos

The only factor changed,
Being your presence,
A lot of change to bear for one small factor,
A lot of acceptance for such less time spent together.

71. Madman

Even, if you were a siren,
I gladly shall listen to your song,
For I know in my bones,
I shall hallucinate of you,
Dream and dread of you.

72. Expectation

My snow flake,
I wish your doubts never got the best of you,
I wish, you walked the path of a daredevil,
Once for the last time,
For I am sure a bed of roses awaits past these thorns.

73. Evocation

I am closely aware,
I hold greater command over my heart,
But my sheer stupidity allows me to clutch
Onto what once was a beautiful memory.
For those memories however minimal,
They were beautiful.

74. Giggle

The biggest of them diamonds hold no value,
Than the pearls spread out through your smile.
Yet I am stranded,
Only to choose them diamonds.

75. Vanquish

I stand at a point where I think,
You do not need much to kill a heart's owned compassion.
Whisper to it about the bright light end of the tunnel,
Let it sit over the thought,
Make the maybe a No.

76. A fool's thought

Love is painful, All consuming,
I felt more hurt in it than out,
Yet I shall gladly jump back into that ditch,
And ponder on for you to drag me out.

77. Longing

I hold a greater anger,
Towards my actions and your thoughts.
The ease of a closed heart no more exists,
Whence it opens,
For numerous emotions rush in and out,
Waiting for it all to fade.

78. Restless

You turned this lover to a child of insomnia,
I certainly know in my bones,
The sleepless nights have less to do with my body,
More in my thoughts those confide in you.

79. Proxy

I have over thought enough,
To let your over-thinking, over-power me,
Yet you over powered my heart to make it bland.
Tis I caused myself to hurt,
But I shall blame you to seek comfort.

80. Caution

I stand afraid to no longer know peace,
With you wandering my heart.
All roads lead to you,
In mind and body.
Fear consumes me,
For I shall do one last stupid thing.

81. Chimera

In your eyes,
I witnessed an entire universe,
And that made me lose interest on the one outside.
Let me dive into them beautiful eyes,
To live the euphoria, I deserve.

82. Recalcitrant

I wondered,
I am gradually getting over you.
Yet all it took was a glance at your reflection,
For the emotions to flood in,
As if there exists no dam.

83. Anticipation

You have made it easy for me,
To forget you placing distance between us.
Yet, I wish you knew the lengths of sacrifice,
I would lay at your feet,
To have you back in my arms.

84. A Promise of Euphoria

My new year's wish,
You moderator of attention,
Why do you listen to your mind over your heart,
When a beautiful elation seeks to crawl around you.

85. Closer But Never Closer

Smite them old souls that ruin your sleep,
For the rest through your travel,
And the tales of it more interesting,
This lonely heart yearns to hear complain again.

86. Eyes to See

I wish you felt the compassion I did towards you,
Or halfway there.
For I am certain, your perspectives would have widened,
Beyond the horizons you thought ever existed.

87. Merit

Be glad,
I have immortalized you over time and space,
For this piece of art shall last beyond you and I.
Yet I wonder if you ever deserve it with the pain,
You shower on me, Through the distance between us.

88. Notability, Lack of it

Beautiful things are happening to me,
Either let in or kept out.
But I no longer find them prominent without you around.
Only If I get to tell you how bad my day went,
Even the worst of them all,
Would still end on a great note.

89. Prediction

I have nearly moved on,
So close,
But when them memories hit,
They hit hard.
Only if you were lesser an idiot,
Yet more reasonable,
We could have salvaged more happiness.

90. Fantasy

I know in certainty,
Your eyes are made of the brightest stars in the cosmos.
I have always worried to glaring longer into them,
Would blind me till I lay asleep forever,
So be it for I'd continue to feel the warmth from them.

91. Decent Down

My bright purple sun,
For I your most loving sunflower,
Shall turn back time before to when I ever bloomed,
If you were to ever set down the horizon.

92. Falsely accused

My Eden's apple,
Why is that I was asked to leave paradise,
For I have not dared to take a bite,
Let alone pluck the fruit,
But only offered to admire the gift of the gods.

93. A Greater Plan

I had you,
I do not anymore,
I had such great joy,
I do not anymore,
Passion overflowed my entity,
It does not anymore,
I know what exactly to be done to recover,
I'm afraid it might not work.

94. Reckoning

Such hard urges I am fighting,
Not to reach you anymore.
Smite me down for missing you much,
Much more than anyone can ever do,
I wish you resonate my ears there is such a path,
I can have you,
Have you around.

95. Boundless, Barrierless

If you were the endless space,
And I what I am,
I would have no moment's hesitation,
To jump into nothingness,
Embrace the cold,
Boil at the surface of your suns,
Wander alone to never be alone,
For an eternity or multiple.

96. Notion

I hold resentment towards everything you were taught,
Of what love was before you met me.
For you felt this thorn protecting you for the rose you are,
To have been poking you.

97. Unease

I have fought no great war,
I have lived through no great depression,
I have witnessed no massacre,
I have sustained no great pain.
But when your thoughts swindle my rice grain for a brain,
I live through them all.

98. Me and My Sleep

I wish, I can talk to you of my dreams,
I wish, I better not dream of you altogether,
But such great scenic I dream of,
Such wonderful things I have been up to in them,
With you.

99. Vexation

I hold courage enough to stand up to an army,
I can fight bare arms with the monster at sea,
I can certainly outrun a bear or two,
But surely worry of competing the feeling,
To never get to see you.

100. Worry

If I was asked to live through the memories with you again,
Or die,
With every strand of my being,
I shall gladly choose death.
For I am more afraid to reach a similar destination,
As this heartache.

101. Thought Fit

I would prefer to bury this eternal sadness,
Which one day would get mild enough to live with,
Rather vanished right away,
For right away had things I had once with you,
To last forever.

102. Unsettled

Madness consumes me, with no regard to time,
Cluelessness has turned to my closest acquaintance,
Comfort my prime foe,
My emotions shattered to every corner to ever exist,
I stand restless to see your confort.

103. Necessitate

I feel such strain on my heart,
As if one has misheld it,
And twisted it with no consideration,
As if one had laid a first glance at it and thrown it away at sea,
I am confused beyond conclusion,
I am lost beyond comprehension,
I am crippled beyond a healthy fix,
I am desperate beyond need,
I am in need,
A clear need of you.

104. Always you

My entire verbiage I throw out at people that know of you
and me,
Is only you,
As classic as it sounds,
I live and breathe you,
I surround and sense you,
You, my living being memory,
You my thriving source of happiness,
I can only not crave much of one,
For you entrail me of a greater adventure of heart than
anyone could ever try.

105. Solitude

Darker and Darker Venom course my veins,
Multiplying madness which never existed.
Tear drops to hug my cheeks forever,
You left me hanging in here.
Sentence me to eternal damnation,
Yet still stick around,
Summon the most disheartened demons on me,
Yet still stick around,
Succumb me to your grace and render me inferior,
Yet still stick around,
Scare me with a generational mustered evil,
Yet still stick around,
Yet still stick around and calm me in your presence.

106. All Over Again

I cannot wait to wake up,
After one long tiring dream,
That lasted for months,
To fix myself to meet you for the first time.

107. It's me

When you find a heart that aches the most,
Walk to it,
I will be there bearing it in my chest,
When you find a mind that worries the most,
Walk to it,
I will be there floating it in my skull.
Walk to it,
For the heart and mind shall seek greater comfort than ever,
forever.

108. Timeless

They say, "If you are lucky, you will come across her who will split time for you. The time before you knew her and the time after."
But dealing with the time, "To never be with her", seems so hard that, I at times wish I never met her.
Would I do it all over again?
Hell Yes.

109. Lighthouse

I no longer own the heart to mask what you make me feel,
Sheer will once allowed me to go through losing you,
Here I stand with scrambled brains to walk towards you,
Or run away from you,
Either thoughts or plans lack to miss considering you,
For I worry, these repercussions may consume me beyond repair,
Yet I still look towards the shore for you to reach the dock.

110. Distraction

Intoxication helps, sometimes not,
Definitely a chance I am willing to take,
For a slightest break from my thoughts about you,
Or simply what I feel from owning them.
Maybe if you are to pull out a maybe,
I would have been fine, Maybe.

111. De Novo

I hope, I can erase all your memories of me,
And keep mine of yours,
So, I can reach out for the first time,
Do this all over for the first time,
Find my way into your heart for the last time.

112. Cupio

A thousand things I wished to do with you,
Now I would settle for one last,
A hundred miles I wished to walk alongside,
Now I would settle for a couple of steps,
A million words I wished to exchange,
Now I would settle for a Hello.

113. Prowess

I think at times or more,
That you never think of what once we were,
Yet I recall your lowest tone,
mentioning how hard it can be on you.
I wish I can muster up the same courage as you,
To choose happiness underived from one's presence.

114. It's Never Right

Too soon, Tad late,
Too much affection, Unsure if we are together,
I do not know much of you, I know who you are.

Filters fall in place of concern, only when you let them concern you.
Isn't it a mere thought that you tell yourself, to push yourself away,
Are you afraid of where the road might lead, or simply unready,
Stop searching for logic through illogical thoughts,
Tell me more of what you think, with an open mind towards speculation,
Let us fix this and progress towards happiness,
Let me pin your mind down and let us overthink together towards togetherness.

115. XX(X)-wn

I cry and weep,
Drain and drown,
Frown for my crown,
Over you hittin' the town,
Do not let my heart down,
Cause I no longer can drown,
Promise me to never letdown,
Let's walk and talk till sundown,
Don't need no breakdown,
Tired of being a clown,
Let's lay-down,
Till moon down
Say no to no, Maybe a Maybe, Be my hometown.

116. Stance

If I were to describe the sound,
That rang my ears, besides continues to grandly with you in thought,
Concerning you and me in the same vicinity,
It would not be a thump or a series on tanggu,
Never a jingle nor my heart itself pounding out.
Rather the sound of the air off a wave, shot off the beach,
Over the curves of paspalum on a sea shore,
Heard with an ear that has been clogged for days,
Vibrant in violets, visualising colours off the sound made from pure thought.
The sound being more imaginary, yet exclusive,
So exclusive that I had to write down for you to listen,
Makes me wonder tis enough to assert compassion towards someone,
Than even bother to waste time, setting pre-norms,
To achieve standard pre-requisites for the foundation of love in itself.
You call me mad and writing the last few lines make me think otherwise.

117. An Assignment Left Behind

In bigger imperfections, I chose to find them little perfect things,
In the chaos of hopelessness, I looked up towards your smile,
You swept me off my feet to rid loneliness, only to abandon me to crawl back into it,
You left me with memories, No one else can match up to,
You etched yourself into my brain, leaving me struggling to forget you.

118. Juger

Anne Sullivan once told Helen Keller "What fool would
think of defeat before even trying?"
And that is all I did to win your compassion.
It was no competition rather a struggle at times,
Only to prove me great women are hard,
I wish you had put me to the test longer and longer,
Maybe one fine day grade me a pass,
But making me quit it, was it fair?
I leave it to you to decide.

119. Intact

I shall find no rest,
Until you are back where you are supposed to be,
Back around me,
Back with me,
Back at me.
I shall yield not to none of the comforts of the home,
Nor surrender my hope,
I may keep up the act of being okay,
But never be okay with you out of my heart,
At all cost, I choose to win you over,
Win your heart and approval.

120. Her and I

A walk down the 100 feet road,
Reminds me of our search for cigarettes and pastries.
An auto ride back home over HAL,
Reminds me of you clutching my arms to rest your head over my shoulder.
I can never take a walk around a lake.
A glance at the corner of Sinan's Street,
Reminds me of the kiss I lay on your forehead before goodbye.
A glimpse of Merin's face,
Traumatizes me over the lack of your presence.
I can never get a tattoo again as long as you roam my heart,
Or let any other woman hint me up with makeup,
Or hold someone's hands or chase them when not held,
Or ask anyone out,
Or open my heart,
Or make new memories that bring great joy,
Or stop thinking of you every waking moment,
Or talk to anyone for hours,
Or crave to do so.

9 798890 660268

Printed by Libri Plureos GmbH in Hamburg,
Germany